THOUGHTS OF A DOMESTIC OBSERVER

SCOTT E. BELBEY

ISBN: 1511455004
ISBN-13: 978-1511455008
Library of Congress Control Number: 2015910027
CreateSpace Independent Publishing Platform
North Charleston, South Carolina

To Candace, for being my strength.
To Hanuman, for keeping me from giving up.
To Bill Maher, because I think we share the same brain.

PREFACE

I kept starting this work with little success. I'd get a few chapters into it, and then I'd quit. I didn't have any excuses, and I didn't really know what to say about it. I had already decided not to give a shit about what anybody else was going to think, so I couldn't really use that as an explanation.

It was frustrating.

I must have spent a week trying to come up with an acceptable reason for why I kept stopping. I was starting to think that I might've been able to write an entire book about why I couldn't write an entire book. That was just stupid enough that I decided to shut up and just get the freaking thing written, regardless of any of the contextual speed bumps I knew I would come across.

Now that I've already gotten through writing the first four chapters, it's finally dawned on me: We'll just skip where I explain how depressing it feels for me to write about why I believe the world is turning to shit. We'll just skip all of that and jump straight to where I explain that there really isn't any feasible way to write a book about this without completely losing at least seven out of every ten readers.

That was my biggest problem. We're discussing a world of people—built by people, controlled by people, and taught by people—who were also taught by the people who came before *them*. This same cycle repeats itself over decades and generations, and yet none of these people have even a clue that some aspects of their passed-down education or guidance might have inexplicably been lost. I tried to cover all of this, and I found myself having to start over again, probably six or seventeen times.

I think I'm done starting over. It's going to be confusing, but I'm still writing this bastard.

CONTENTS

Preface v

Acknowledgments ix

1. Society...1

2. To Protect...3

3. Environment..7

4. Health Care (for Tamika)...10

5. Wealth...13

6. To Serve..16

7. Plutocracy 20

8. Education..23

9. Religion...26

10. Balance 31

About the Author 35

ACKNOWLEDGMENTS

I'd like to take a moment to acknowledge each and every executive and politician I might have called out for doing something reckless and irresponsible to our planet. Pick a cheek and pucker up, folks.

Chapter 1
SOCIETY

Allow me to take a moment and clarify that when I mention the *world*, I'm referring specifically to our society. When I'm talking about our society, I'm referring to the United States of America. I bring this up only because our country has its flaws, and I believe these flaws are at least indirectly responsible for the problems we constantly have to deal with.

Before we get any further into this, I think it's important that I mention my lack of a higher education. I'm not a genius, I don't play one on television, and all I have to share with you are the speculations of an imperfect man who tries to pay close attention to what he watches, reads, or hears. You're almost better off thinking of me only as a neglected boyfriend who has to sit through every episode of *Project Runway* because his girlfriend probably loves it more than she loves him. In other words, I'm not an expert on the human condition. I'm only a reluctant observer.

I suppose most of you wish to know what I'm talking about. Yes, it's true that I've said society has its problems and that those problems are behind whatever brand of misery our citizens suffer. That's just freaking terrific, but it goes much deeper than that. I'm willing to concede that it isn't actually the idea or the intention of society to make the human race miserable. I'm also willing to acknowledge that society's main purpose has always been to keep us civilized. Conversely, it should also be pointed out that society is an achievement of humankind, and the human race has always been far from perfect.

I have to be honest about this. I've been taking notes in preparation for writing this thing. Of course I've included the general subject matter, the direction that I'm taking this, and a few examples here and there that most of us would be hard-pressed to argue with, and—not to put too fine a point on it—I'm beginning to scare the crap out of myself.

Keeping this on track, I think I would like to go back to my last point, which is that the goal of society is at least partly to keep us civilized. Somebody close to me has recently suggested that I think too much, and I think she might be right. This brings to mind an interesting notion that I'd like to suggest: I don't believe we're making any further efforts to civilize ourselves.

In fact, I suggest that the human race (for the most part) believes that we've finished baking in that regard. I feel this way because our focus has been (again, for the most part) on developing only new innovations that make our lives easier rather than keeping our attention on ways to make it easier for the human race to live better. Yes, there is a difference between the two.

We've put far too much focus on the widest televisions. The sleekest pocket computers (I used to call them cell phones) are all the rage, and we seem to love commercials that offer us a sneak peek at how long we get to wait before starting payments on a car as expensive as a large home from the early 1960s.

We care too much about our toys when we should probably care more about becoming better people. In that same vein, I'm sure I wouldn't surprise anybody if I suggested that there is a connection between the amount of money we spend on useless crap and how most of us feel about ourselves. It's my belief, and in some ways my experience, that instead of making an effort to improve ourselves, we still choose to distract ourselves with expensive things we don't actually need—as if our society didn't already have enough distractions (which I'll talk about a little later).

Chapter 2
TO PROTECT

I often think about that famous motto we see on the police interceptors. "To serve and protect" used to mean something to us. (Yes, I'm sure it still does to many.) Allow me to back up for a moment and explain that I haven't any desire to pick on our civil servants. That isn't why I brought this up. Whether it's to serve and protect, or to protect and serve, I think the same motto applies to all of our civil servants. City employees behind glass wish only to help—otherwise, they would have found another line of work. Their motivations are selfless, and each of them should be honored for his or her service. A large portion of this book isn't going to be a constant chorus of happy puppies and children running around belching laughter and farting sunshine, because the motto we've seen on our police interceptors can apply directly to society as a whole. The problem is that with society, it takes on an entirely different and more insidious meaning.

Society is meant to protect us, but the only thing it (or we) need protection from is ourselves. This kind of protection is focused more on society's short-term survival and less on its long-term preservation. Whether some acknowledge this or not doesn't matter; it only becomes more valid as our infrastructure begins to crumble, our drinking water becomes toxic, and the air we breathe begins to smell like baked vomit.

I'm sure nobody wishes to read a book about the possible end of days, and I'm also sure that many people will read this with the automatic belief that I'm just an idiot. It's human. I can't blame anybody, but thoughts like these are real, and I very much doubt that I'm the only person thinking them.

Close this book and stop reading if you must. Complain to everybody you know the next time you're in church. Don't listen to whatever this scary writer just told you in his (oh-so-terrible) book of lies. Relax yourself with whatever brand of comfort you might need. You'll not hear any objections from my end. We're all entitled to whatever peace or comfort we can find, and I've no desire to make anybody miserable. That particular damage is already being done, whether or not this book gets written. It isn't my fault that correcting society's mistakes will always cost the country far more than it takes to make them, which automatically means that we're always going to keep ourselves behind the proverbial Eight Ball of Doom.

If you need an example, how about our cars? It doesn't seem to matter to anybody how dependent our society has become on automobiles that burn fossil fuels. It frightens me that we've grown so dependent on fossil fuels, and I somehow doubt that our economy would survive if that particular well ever dried up.

While we're on this subject, it also bothers me to absolutely no end that hybrids seem to be considered the only real solution. I won't get into how expensive they are, but it seems that they're only being hailed as something viable by consumers because of how rarely we need to fill up the gas tank. It also bothers me how often I hear other people tell me that they won't purchase either a hybrid or an electric car, because of the amount of coal or fossil fuel that the power grid might be burning for the electricity to recharge them. That particular reasoning appears valid on the surface, but many people use it only as an excuse. Most of them are still shuffling papers at work under the same lights that their city burns coal or oil for. Most of those people are also not planning any political movements to convince our elected officials to switch the city to a more sustainable source of power.

The need to bitch, complain, and yet not lift a finger to do anything to address the problem is what I call a symptom of apathy, and this apathy is yet another reason why I decided to write this. Whether or not it's doing it on purpose, our society sustains this apathy. If you need another explanation, I can accommodate you.

Humanity will not acknowledge things that it doesn't care about. By that same token, we also can't bring ourselves to care about things we have no control over. This is the cause of our apathy, and it's at least partly responsible for almost every problem that our society has created for itself—the major one being the cars that we drive.

As another example, I feel that the US government has acted negligently in regards to our laws on gun control, meaning that we've done very little on a national level to prevent further gun-related tragedies. Regardless of the excuses, it's most likely a common-enough opinion that greed, pressure from special interests, and a general insensitivity toward what all of the related victims have been through have been the causes. If anything might create that apathy on a level I can't even begin to consider, it would be the continued evidence that we the people have no control over how we're governed. Either that, or we're allowed too much control, and there are too many idiots or fools out there.

I sincerely and deeply apologize for not mentioning all the gun-related victims by name, but our freedom—as it relates to the use and ownership of firearms in the United States—was originally granted by the Second Amendment to the US Constitution (or Amendment IV to our Bill of Rights) to help all of its citizens feel safe and secure, but that was over two hundred years ago. Now, a large number of us are ignorant, selfish, paranoid sociopaths. It is for that reason alone that the citizens, or at least those taught well enough to know better, should feel anything but safe and secure.

This is one of the many reasons why I think our society needs a wake-up call, but there are several more. I will not be trying to list all of them because I don't think anybody would wish to read a 10,731-page book. Also, I really don't wish to write one.

What I haven't told you and will mention now is that we're currently living in a great land of confusion. We go through the motions, often more than blissfully ignorant of the fact that we're being led or guided by a world full of right hands that don't know or give a shit about what the left hands are up to. I cannot write a book about the problems that we've created for ourselves without causing myself some stress. Anyway, the point I was trying to make is that our society is protecting itself but only by ensuring its short-term survival. There are several reasons why this isn't going to work. Let's say that some poor fool decides he or she has gotten tired of being broke and decides to rob a bank. The efforts we've made to ensure our short-term survival would cover that, so of course we would manage to arrest or kill the broke idiot. We would also manage to recover some hostages, and then we'd attend a memorial service for the hostages we couldn't save. Why aren't we looking into why the idiot was broke in the first place?

Was he or she unemployed?

Why?

Did he or she slip through one of the many cracks in our current educational system?

Why?

It isn't that we've proved ourselves incapable of asking such questions, because we obviously *have* to ask them. The victims—or their families—demand it of us. I think that our problem is only that we live in the land of the free, which means that even if we ask all the right questions, we're still free to leave the difficult answers for another time or free to leave the problem for some other unlucky asshole who comes along a year or two later. It also means that we're free to completely ignore the problem until it cripples our way of life.

Chapter 3
ENVIRONMENT

I think one of the reasons I've avoided this chapter (considering that I've written almost seven chapters before getting back to this one) is that I'm not a scientist. I don't even want to pretend that I'm a scientist and that I know what I'm talking about. It shows a complete and total lack of respect toward the individuals who did indeed go through university and who do indeed know what the fuck they're talking about. Having said that, I think it's that very disdain or lack of respect that I need to write about. There is something to be said for common sense because it is my feeling that we might have lost it. When the majority of our scientific minds insist that we are causing an impending disaster, I don't believe that our elected officials were ever selected for their ability to ignore the science or for their ability to use their supposedly superior scientific intellects to debate it.

Even if our government of fools managed to pay off just a minority of scientists to offer an argument against the threats of implied doom that we're being warned of, one might think that even just our *potential* risk of disaster would be too great to ignore. This is where I believe that our common sense should have stepped in and taken the reins. One might have thought that our minds would still be sharp enough to realize that the oil industries do not care about our planet or the life that walks upon it. I'm not an idiot, but I'm also not a rocket scientist in the world of business. Even somebody with my lack of formal education should be smart enough to realize that the oil industry has no reason to care. There's no friggin' profit in it.

Don't even get me started on our politicians. A great number of our elected officials are already so old that many of them will probably die of old age before they get to see the results of any of their disastrous errors in judgment.

I don't think this chapter is about the environment, specifically. As I've already said, I'm not a scientist. I won't act like one, but what I do wish to write about are all the assholes responsible. Here's my biggest issue: I'm willing to entertain the notion that some members of our government are accepting some form of bribe or disbursement from the oil industries, but let's be honest—whether we like it or not, we're living in a society that revolves around money, and we already know that our politicians are human. The very notion that some of them act like morons or as if they've got their heads in the sand (at least to me) indicates that they've been coerced not to vote in anybody's best interests but their own.

But you know what? I'll hold my bitching about politics until later. I don't wish to waste this entire chapter blaming our different political parties. I think it would be too easy, and they've done enough already that I can blame them for. I'd rather take this moment to blame everybody else. That's right. Each and every single one of us can be blamed. Each of us is responsible for the state of our planet. All of us throw our trash in the kitchen garbage, oblivious to the fact that the trash bag isn't biodegradable or that it's possibly gonna go to a dump somewhere to fester and be choked on by raccoons. I already mentioned our apathy. I apologize if that's the case, but both the state of our planet and our collective lack of common sense are the results of it. There are a number of mistakes we've made throughout our history. It wasn't that we knew; it's that we know *now*, and yet we still allow it to continue. I think about every careless move that we as a species make against both our planet and our future. There are times when I wonder whether or not we truly deserve survival because we should know better. That's what I believe is our biggest flaw, and it pisses me off. We are supposed to know better, and yet we indirectly cause our polar ice caps to melt by allowing a collection of toxic industries not only to continue, but also to flourish. I'm speaking not only of the oil industry but also the automotive industry. We can't have one without the other, but which came first? It's the old classic and frightening chicken-and-egg argument.

I think that it ultimately doesn't matter which came first. Let's be honest with one another. In almost every conceivable way that we can look at it, oil is *death*. This cannot only be interpreted that way because of the notion that oil is a fossil fuel, but let's take a look at oil for a moment. It's black, it's murky, it smells terrible, and drinking it is a horrible idea. Bathing in it is also terrible, so leave the robe on. Apart from the benefit we get for burning the shit out of it, oil offers nothing apart from pollutants in our atmosphere. Now, it's true that I've said or implied that oil is death—probably too many times already—but this particular argument isn't ridiculous because we keep having it. It's fucking ridiculous that we keep needing to. We are flirting with (and making accommodations for) death by allowing the continued manufacture or use of any combustion engine. It's that simple. I'm not going to sugarcoat this. We're probably killing ourselves, our children, our neighbors, their children, and the possibility of not only any future generations' happiness but also their very existence.

I really don't wish to tell everybody how to live their lives. What I will suggest is that, whether we want it or not, we have a responsibility to care for our home and all of the beasts that we share it with. From up here at the top of the food chain, we have a responsibility to all of the animals below us. It's up to us to make sure that we still have a food chain. As the lord of our jungles, we should be showing all of our subjects that we weren't put above them simply to abuse, kill, or put them on the endangered-species list.

Animals hunt other animals for food. Animals kill for survival, and that's natural. Meanwhile, only man kills or maims other animals for their tusks, fangs, claws, or even their balls. Animals wouldn't consider us one of their own, and they certainly wouldn't call us gods. Had they the ability, they would call us monsters.

Chapter 4
HEALTH CARE (FOR TAMIKA)

This is yet another one of the chapters that I didn't wish to write. This is more than likely because my wife's sister has ovarian cancer. Maybe it's also because she had evidently beaten it once already, but was later blown off or ignored by her supposed health care providers when she proactively told them she felt like she needed a checkup. Now, we have since learned that the cancer has metastasized—spread out across her body—and has reached one of her lungs. As far as medical insurance goes, it's my understanding that she currently has COBRA (Consolidated Omnibus Budget Reconciliation Act). Tamika isn't even thirty, so I don't know what to say. I keep wanting to punch something, but all I can really do is pray for her and dedicate this chapter to both her and to others like her. It occurs to me that the larger our population becomes, the greater the number of people we'll see with illnesses we can't cure. It's a reasonable concern.

I was pleased when President Obama set up the Affordable Care Act. I voted for him in both presidential elections because I believe he cares about the country. I was pleased that he proved it by making medical insurance easier to get and more affordable for everybody who needs it. However, it bothers me (more than a little) that we have to depend on medical insurance, and it also bothers me that Obamacare was simply chosen as the "next best thing" solution after single-payer or universal health care.

I've gotten very tired of hearing about the Republican Congress's constant struggle to have the Affordable Care Act repealed because it's un-American, too socialist, Obama isn't white enough, or we can't afford it. Our country acts like the wealthiest superpower on the planet—up to the point where we need to help our own citizens. We throw millions of dollars around just to save Wall Street from a take-over or to rescue banks when they've been caught doing something greedy or stupid. We still spend a horrifically huge fortune on our military-industrial complex. Smaller countries like Cuba have universal health care, whether or not they can afford it, because they know the difference between being human and being a dick. They probably won't be making huge fortunes anytime soon. Yet they still offer universal health care. What am I missing?

I remember discussions in the classroom about the evils of communism. I remember being taught that capitalism was the "bestest-ever system in the whole wide world!" When I was a child, I remember being told that our way of life was the preferred model. Meanwhile, communists recognize the human right to stay alive while our health care system only recognizes that some asshole somewhere needs to profit from a person's physical misfortune.

Our Declaration of Independence describes life, liberty, and the pursuit of happiness as our unalienable rights. Most importantly, *life* is listed first. I've never noticed anything in parentheses mentioning that it wasn't supposed to be the most important just because it was listed before *liberty*.

If we were to look up *unalienable* or *inalienable* in a thesaurus, we would find words like *essential, fundamental, ingrained, implicit, genetic, intrinsic,* and *fixed*. The *Merriam-Webster Online Dictionary* defines it as "impossible to take away or give up," while Vocabulary.com suggests that "what's unalienable cannot be taken away or denied." There isn't anything I can find suggesting that we have to pay through the nose for it or that the cost of it might be so high that certain unfortunate people must simply die if they can't pay their medical bills.

All of this pisses me off because, as with almost everything else that I feel the need to bitch or rant about in this work, I'm having a hard time believing that the United States cares about its citizens. Don't get me wrong. Individuals care about other individuals, but large-enough groups of us suck. I can't explain it any better than that. I'm a pretty simple man. Given a choice between saving the lives of even the strangers or fools around me or having money, I'd rather be broke and save lives. It feels to me as though there's a broken fuse somewhere in the upper echelons of our humanity, and the damage that it's caused can't become any more conspicuous than it already has within the US government.

Chapter 5
WEALTH

I used to live in a southern state. While I could spend an enormous amount of time talking about how righteous or bitchin' it was, I'd rather not. I'm sure all of you know bullshit when you hear it. I think it's important to mention that it isn't the entire state or its elected officials that I'm trying to pick on. Everything I write about this particular state is fueled by the impressions I formed as a small child. Though I have no idea whether anything has actually changed, I'm still willing to acknowledge the possibility.

The first and most memorable impression I got from living in this state, besides the often-reinforced and abhorrent opinion that redneck Christian kids hated Jewish kids for not being Christian, was from our drives to the beach. As the drive went on over the thirty or so minutes that it took to hit the sand, I was constantly kept silent by how awful the neighborhoods gradually became during the drive. It was like some terrible scenic tour of impoverished horror. There were several questions I found myself wanting to ask, regardless of how many times the trip was repeated or how many times I received a bullshit answer. I would often wonder why nobody wanted to clean up the empty buildings or boarded-up storefronts. I would always wonder why anybody would bother with white paint when somebody else would always tag the walls with crude signatures. Then I'd always wonder why the African-Americans I saw walking from one building to the next never got fed.

No. We're not going to discuss how terrible that sounds because I already know. I wasn't even a teenager back then. Like all of us, I was a product of my environment. As always seems to be the case, we're discussing an environment in a perpetual state of ignorance and decay. It was that environment that I most remembered, and I was rarely exposed to anything but the worst that its citizens had to offer.

I won't argue with all of the brainiacs in our world who might disagree with this, but it's my opinion that the more wealth we put into building something, the more wealth we need to maintain it or keep it standing. I believe that this is the cause of decay that we often have to contend with in our society. It's a constant problem, and it's one shared by all colors and creeds throughout our world.

It's about wealth and what's being done with it. I don't believe that wealth is necessarily evil, but how it's shared isn't exactly awesome. While we have one or two dozen people managing to make billions, we also have billions of people barely scraping by. I might agree that many lazy people are only broke because they never reached their full potential, but it's our society's wealth that has failed to assist our public schools in reaching their own. It's the students who suffer these shortcomings, and it's going to be our society's future that suffers as a result.

Wealth can be a positive constant in our lives. It has always been used as a measurement of how much an individual has accomplished, and this has never been a bad thing. I think our main problems are the lengths that we go to and the focus that we have in order to make more of it.

I think it's ridiculous and oddly perverse that the bulk of our poorly educated masses just accept this nation's increasingly unnecessary shortcomings and can only protect themselves with bullshit catchphrases like "it's the American way," or "if you don't like it here, get out." We'll just forget for the moment that a large percentage of the poor probably couldn't afford to leave.

Regardless, many of our current problems are connected with one another. People often lose their jobs because of the constant pursuit of profit that makes it more attractive for our companies or corporations to leave the United States and take advantage of lower wages elsewhere or take advantage of new technology that makes employees unnecessary.

I was a child when the company my father worked for went batshit crazy. A pseudo–investment banker named Frank Lorenzo bought Eastern Airlines and began to sell pieces of the airline for profit, despite the fact that it was still in operation. The end result was that hundreds, if not thousands, of people ended up out of work.

I get tired of everybody blaming the wealthy for what's wrong with the world. No, I'm not wealthy. No, I'm not taking sides. I agree that some of the wealthy use what they have to influence political decisions, and they will sometimes pay a fortune to get what they want. However, I disagree that the rest of us are blameless. The apathy that all of us suffer from is very real, and it prevents us from playing a positive role in our society. Maybe the rich *can* be selfish. Maybe they *can* cause problems, but the middle-class or poor who've allowed it to continue (since we outnumber the wealthy by probably a million to one) should accept some of the blame.

Regardless, how either group conducts itself isn't really so important. There are exceptions to this, but neither the rich or the poor look beyond their own interests; like everything else I've already mentioned, it's completely human to be selfish. I believe that what many do not consider is that, unlike our debt, our wealth is built from a finite resource. Our population continues to grow. The amount of wealth we need in order to maintain everything is also going to increase. While I'm perfectly willing to entertain how completely incorrect I might be, any arguments I receive would likely fail to explain the decay and poverty that I was forced to observe just on a drive to the coast as a little boy.

Chapter 6
TO SERVE

We've already spoken briefly about the motto "To serve and protect" and how those words apply to society. I've already mentioned how I think we protect our more immediate future while ignoring the distant future that we should always be preparing for. I won't rehash what I've said previously; instead, I'd like to explain where the *serve* part comes in. Whether or not it's being done on purpose, society serves itself by serving all of us the distractions that prevent us from contemplating what we're missing in our lives. I need to explain something important. In life, I don't believe that our problems are as important as the solutions. If we were to truly examine this, I believe we might find that a great number of our current problems are only so prevalent because we aren't courageous enough to take the necessary steps to solve them. I could probably write an entirely new chapter just about that, but I won't bother.

We are being distracted. To begin with, please tell me what goal a television is supposed to accomplish. Beyond providing emergency services, babysitting toddlers when we're on the phone, or receiving possible messages from our government, what service can it offer apart from sports or entertainment? I somehow doubt that we're keeping it for its unbiased news. While we're on that particular subject, doesn't the bias that we've seen or witnessed offer its own distractions?

I'm hearing a television right now as I'm writing this. My wife is watching *Reign*. I always feel bad that I don't wish to join her. I can't spend any long periods of time on my ass. I can't just sit around in front of a television without feeling compelled to move around and accomplish something. I was diagnosed with multiple sclerosis in February of 2007. As far as sitting on my butt goes, sometimes I don't have much choice. So when I do have a choice, I'm doing something productive.

When I consider the television, I can't prevent myself from thinking about all of the unfortunate people who spend far too much time on the couch gaining all of the weight that they probably won't be able to lose. The television has always been a double-edged sword. We're talking about a medium that allows thousands or millions of people within the entertainment or commercial industries to make their fortunes while, at the same time, giving millions of other people an excuse to just watch television after a long day at work, when they might have chosen to succeed in life instead. They would rather sit their asses down and get their fill of often-partisan news programming or stupid one-liners before they go to sleep, wake up, and go back to work again. Many distractions like our televisions have been affecting our development as a society for a long time.

Another example is our game systems. I laugh whenever I imagine how each company responsible for our games might eventually have to develop a virtual-reality system in which the real world is replaced, and the only things we're aware of that are real are the other players who have signed in with us. I then imagine children putting on their VR goggles, VR gloves, and maybe their VR boots. I imagine siblings beginning a mixed martial-arts game—shortly before they are taken to a real-life hospital because they've inadvertently beaten the real-life crap out of one another.

I won't be writing about whether or not violent video games teach children that violence is an acceptable way to solve disagreements. That's always going to be a problem because, regardless of how great the parents might be, they can't effectively teach their children if the kids lock themselves up in their bedrooms to shoot up a pixelated shopping mall.

I believe our real problem is one of endurance or stamina. Most of us spending any real amount of time on a game system probably don't have much. I'm also talking about the intellectual endurance or stamina that each of us is supposed to have. I grew up during the beginning of the electronic-game era. Whether or not there are experts out there who might argue this point, I know from personal experience that it's always going to be preferable to play a game rather than learn what we're being taught by the adults that guide us through our childhoods. While it's true that we've always had that struggle between work and play standing in the way of our growth, we've had to sit back and witness the inevitable defeat of the adults in that struggle.

I meant it when I called it a *struggle*, and all of us know it. The United States has been suffering from an obesity problem, and the corporations behind our game systems are so aware of their role in it that they've tried to produce and promote games that encourage some physical exertion from the players. What I find truly ironic is that the physical exertion these games encourage is in many ways probably less than half the exertion that the kids have already given up to play these games in the first place.

Our games are only a small part of it because we almost *encourage* the continued intellectual apathy of our children by allowing their possession of pocket computers (i.e., cell phones) in school. We've been led (or programmed) to believe that these pocket computers are absolutely necessary for our children's safety—despite the fact that most of us had to go to and from school long before these phones were on the market. I could probably write yet another chapter on just how difficult these devices have made it for teachers to do their jobs. Do we really think our kids won't use the calculator to solve a math problem? Do we truly believe playing *Angry Chickens* won't be regarded as an option the moment a history lesson in class begins to bore the crap out of students? Are we dumb, or are we just too busy with life to give a shit? This is an especially sore point for me because my wife is a struggling teacher.

The Internet came about after Russia sent its first satellite into space, and Eisenhower put a think tank together for working on new ideas. This think tank began work on creating the first network of different computers. I think the main idea was that, should they be linked together, two computers could solve the same problem faster than only one. The effort was obviously a success, but what price have we paid as a result of it?

It occurs to me that we might be more likely to remember a fact if we had made an effort to find it or look it up in an encyclopedia or book. All we need to do now is use a search engine. With the ease with which we're able to find information over the web, it seems somewhat unlikely to me that any libraries will exist after 2030.

In addition to this, considering the constant online or television advertisements for the various dating sites on the Internet, it seems unlikely that anybody will grow up believing in the value of taking one's time to meet new people, make friends, and eventually sleep with one after confirming compatibility. The biggest lesson we as a society will ultimately learn is that our wives, husbands, girlfriends, or boyfriends are essentially disposable. The first argument any of you have will break you up, because what the hell—each of you is easily replaced.

While we're talking about this new world of relationship bliss that we've created for ourselves, let's also take a moment to lower our heads and give silent thanks to the Internet for the free and unlimited porn. Have you ever seen a movie so many times that you ended up hating it? Whether anybody wishes to acknowledge this or not, I've learned through personal experience that the same thing applies to lifestyles and preferences in pornography. Because my disability often keeps me at home, I've been forced by my gradual but inevitable boredom to move on to other things. That reminds me, I'd like to assure readers that no cowboys, clowns, supermodels, U-boat captains, Vikings, or cartoon characters were harmed in the making of the porno that I just finished. Thanks, Ike, for the Internet!

I think it's also important that I mention another issue I have with the Internet. It's simple. It's that everybody has access. Absolutely everybody is free to post their thoughts or opinions for the rest of the world to read. Unfortunately, many of these people probably shouldn't have bothered. Our thoughts or opinions can come off as ignorant, self-involved, immature, or dangerous. We're talking about millions of people who use the Internet in an effort to set themselves apart from everybody else. As a result, what happens is that those who have a real thought or notion worth repeating get buried and lost underneath all of the bullshit. We're not in danger of being distracted by the Internet as much as we're in danger of getting lost in the idiocy.

Chapter 7
PLUTOCRACY

Let's examine what we're talking about. Our society seems to encourage extremes when it comes to differences in income but only prefers it when a small percentage manages to beat the system and reach for the brass ring. This means that the poor will always greatly outnumber the wealthy, and the education of our children is being tailored (whether or not it's being done on purpose) to protect us from the horrifying risks of upward mobility. Yes, I was just being sarcastic.

"Upward mobility" is a phrase heard from both political parties. It refers to the upward climb each of us can supposedly make from one social class into another. It's usually a dream because what we're really talking about are examples like the broke becoming rich, the ignorant becoming well schooled, and things of that nature. It's a wonderful story that usually ends well before we've woken up and blinked at the ceiling. While the United States might still preach that everybody in the country can succeed and live that dream, our country's *foundation* (I love using that word) of freedom and success has done nothing but crumble for decades.

I won't point any fingers (or flip any birds), but I believe our current problems began with the Republican Party's belief that a smaller government should be running the country. It is this belief that fuels the conservative need to deregulate absolutely everything that keeps the country grounded or safe from itself.

But I don't want to spend any additional time discussing political parties. I'm obviously not as well versed as others. What I really intended to write about are the changes that I think all of us have noticed but have probably ignored. Whether or not we've conquered our apathy and stepped up to the plate to change things, it would seem that our Republic and the supposed democracy that controls it have been bought and sold by our nation's wealthy.

Am I nuts? Am I jumping the gun and maybe inciting a little bit of panic? Maybe I am, and I apologize for that. I'll acknowledge the possibility that I'm full of shit, but I'll tell you something. It doesn't matter if I'm correct or not because reality is perception's little bitch, and whether or not what I say is true, we've already seen more than enough evidence that I know what I'm ranting about.

It's like what I mentioned earlier. Gun control? (Pfft!) It doesn't matter how many schools get gunned down because the National Rifle Association pays—and pays well. It doesn't matter how toxic our environment becomes because our oil industry pays even better. It also doesn't matter how bad the quality of our education becomes or how quickly our infrastructure crumbles because the wealthy are always going to get out of paying their fair share.

You can debate this as hard or as often as you wish because the wealthy don't need to own us. They don't need to own us or own the government. Even just the idea of wealth already controls every aspect of our lives.

What's truly horrific about all of this is that we've made them wealthy. It's the 99 percent of the population (the poor) that supports the remaining 1 percent by purchasing all of their useless crap or services. Come to think of it, that might be part of the reason why our wealthy try so hard to get out of paying their fair share of taxes. They wouldn't want our public education to get any better because they need as many ignorant people among us as possible. Having too many intelligent people living in our country might hurt their bottom line.

Here is where I backtrack a little and remind you of what I've said earlier about the wealthy. I don't actually blame them. I'm not saying that they're blameless so much as I'm saying that they're clueless. Most of our corporations are so compartmentalized that they probably almost run themselves. The wealthy executives are most likely too busy playing with their wealth to either notice or give a shit.

This is where I need to suggest to everybody that some additional time needs to be taken. What I'm proposing is that we examine our world and our place in it. We should spend some time analyzing the real differences between *want* and *need* because far too many dollars are spent satisfying our thirst for things we never needed.

Remember all of the words I spewed in discussing distractions? That's what I'm talking about. If you're just buying shit because it's gonna look righteous in your living room or everybody else has one (so why not), then all you're doing is distracting yourself. It's an indication of weakness and apathy, and it won't make you happy.

Here's another shock for you.

Wake up. Happiness has never been a permanent state of mind. If it had been, none of us would have ever known enough to fully appreciate it. Contentment is what everybody should be shooting for—except that we're missing a vital component that I feel is truly important. The wealthy and their aforementioned distractions have been keeping us from seeing it.

That's why I believe that we should learn to acknowledge the very real differences between what we want and what we need. Focusing only on what we need might eventually reshape things for the better.

Chapter 8
EDUCATION

I used to work at a store that sold recliners. I enjoyed selling the product because I believed in the store's signature brand. I never thought I was a fantastic salesman, but I know I was at least helpful enough to keep myself employed. There was a lot of downtime, which I spent reading all of the books or issues of *National Geographic* that the showroom had on display with their living-room sets. There were a few books that I managed to read from cover to cover. Believe it or not, the most interesting of these books was an American history textbook used during the early 1940s. It was published in the '30s, if I remember correctly. The biggest reason I had for continuing to read this book was that I was surprised by its content. I remember reading a chapter about the fears that our government had regarding the state of our economy after the last of our Founding Fathers passed away. I was stunned by how insightful that was. It was with that book that the history of the United States of America was being taught in school—in a way that provoked a need for emotional growth, intelligence, and critical thinking—and it practically dared all of us to question everything we'd been told. I loved that book, but I was also horrified by it.

What the hell could have happened? I remember world history when I was in junior high or American history when I was in high school. With either of these books, names and dates were shared in a way suggesting that memorizing something was much more important than actually learning it. I couldn't help but wonder what else our education might have lost. Now it's being suggested that something as pedestrian and normal as cursive handwriting might be phased out of our current curricula, and I shudder to think what might be next.

What we're discussing isn't the money that our states put into public schools. Regardless of the intentions of the government and the money that they may or may not spend, our educational system is obviously in trouble. From what I've observed, it's been struggling for several years. The first, and probably most important, aspect that I think we're missing in our schools is the attention and enthusiasm of the students. Such losses (in my opinion) are born partly from the latent resentment of children, who know that they have little choice or say in the matter. While we're on that subject, we can also go back to our game systems again. If we were to consider that for a moment, we would probably realize that for a long time, learning something new has no longer been fun. This will always be the case when we compare school to the games kids can play. It's also not awesome that so many of these kids already have a reason to believe that, like their parents before them, they're probably not going to succeed in life.

I'm not an expert on education. I won't pretend otherwise, but I'm writing these particular thoughts and observations because I'm at least smart enough to realize how important our kids are and how dangerous it is for us to diminish their future. I could very easily just continue with my current pattern of indirectly and passive-aggressively blaming the wealthy for absolutely everything. I could throw a few choice insults their way. I could blame conservative politicians for making it too easy for our wealthy to execute their master plan of turning 99 percent of our population into a vast pool of pissed-off and ignorant wage slaves held under the thumbs of our country's remaining 1 percent. I can do that (because I kinda want to), but I won't (dammit).

My biggest concern right now is that I think we've shot ourselves in the foot. I've already said that we live in a land of the free (even though our prison populations might suggest otherwise). It's the existence of these freedoms that has made it too easy for companies to sell their distractions and make a profit. Regrettably, though I won't point any fingers at any company specifically, it's also been made too easy for our children to let these distractions impact their studies and possibly (in a few cases) their mental or emotional growth.

Our children have much more to worry about than just their distractions. I could spend a great deal of time discussing our teachers because the pay that teachers receive is abhorrent. If annual salaries are any indication, I'd have to suggest that most taxpayers look upon public schools as free day care centers, and teachers are the babysitters. How can we expect our teachers to do as great a job as they might have originally intended when most of them are still forced to live from paycheck to paycheck?

How are our children supposed to do as great a job in school as possible and grow up to become productive members of society when their schools, teachers, general education, and overall future are not shown the respect they deserve? I was never a great student when I was in school, but despite how I might have felt as an obnoxious teenager, my outlook has since changed. I don't think I'm completely wrong in suggesting to everybody that our halls of education should be honored. They should be held to a higher standard and should be much easier to access. They should be palaces with unlimited resources and plenty of happy teachers.

My biggest regret about my old job was that I never bought that old history textbook from the showroom.

Chapter 9
RELIGION

I have no problem with religion. I think the belief in a higher power—and the belief that said higher power loves us—is a beautiful, healthy, and potent thing. The issues that I have are only with the people responsible when the religion's basic idea becomes twisted and ugly. Every time an effort has been made to rekindle what we need, people have ended up inadvertently taking it away from us. Jesus of Nazareth (as an example) only wished to be a source of strength and love for his people—until the elders arranged for his crucifixion by the Romans. After Jesus became a martyr, an entire church, or religion, was built. It wasn't built upon the guidance that he offered those who heard his words but upon the foundation of loss leftover from his crucifixion (hence the cross being used as a horrific, universal symbol). Jesus of Nazareth became known as Jesus Christ, and the church built with a name that he was never born with gradually became a global power.

Awesome—except that the emotional and spiritual support that this religion offers has always been provisional, depending on whether Christians continue obeying their church. It has also been suspect, considering the belief that the flock go to a better place after they've passed on—provided that each individual can die as a good and obedient Christian.

It isn't my place to argue dogma, so I won't. It doesn't matter to me at all that even two or three hundred years after the crucifixion, most churches decided that they knew what happened after death or assumed that they knew how the universe was created. It doesn't matter that people were trained or programmed to believe what they were told, that *faith* became another word for *gullibility*, and, despite the vague certainty that most religious people were armed with, most of us still thought that the friggin' earth was flat.

Despite everything you've just read, I meant it when I expressed my earlier belief that religion is supposed to be a positive thing for humanity. There was a time in my life when having something to believe in became paramount for me, and the number of speed bumps during this personal exploration weren't making my search an easy one. My experience with Judaism as a child soured things for me. I didn't wish to be a Christian, despite the disturbingly large number of unfaithful married women who tried to relax their throats while failing to use their claws and yank me into the fold. I ultimately turned my back on all of the Abrahamic religions, regardless of the high regard I might have had for Muslims (yes, you heard that correctly) and the clarity with which they offer their love and respect for Allah. While I'll always envy their purity and level of commitment, I still decided, sometime after September 11, 2001, that some of the more radical ones needed to go and get their shit sorted out. Either way, I don't believe that it's Islam that's the problem. I didn't believe that it was ever the religion. As with everything that we've often dealt with, it's the people and their environment that we need to keep an eye on.

I spent some additional time looking into Hinduism, Taoism, and Wicca, and I even spent time attending meetings with the Society of Friends. The conclusion that I eventually reached was that only the support I've gained through selfless action and personal perseverance can keep me at the level of strength that I need. Anything else is a poor substitute.

I believe that one of our greatest flaws is the tendency to see religion as a means with which we might gain additional wealth, power, or authority over others. This particular brand of power isn't something we can just dismiss, if we consider all of the hate and death that it's been responsible for. I won't bring up any examples. It's been done on countless occasions, and yet I already know that hate and death are going to continue.

Regardless, people have a hunger for spiritual strength and support, whether they realize what they're truly missing or not, so of course they're going to wish to sustain whatever metaphysical or spiritual well they're currently drinking from. The masses are going to listen to their church ministers pull from a very old book, borrow whatever wisdom they believe is still relevant, and then tell them what they're supposed to believe—just so the church can help the attending public feel secure with the world and their place in it.

I think another one of the issues I have is that the benefit we receive in church is always fleeting. It's so temporary that we have to go back and hear more a week later. I take that as a sign that what these institutions offer isn't meant to last—either that, or our society is just so screwed up that there isn't anything that any minister can share that can truly set our minds or hearts at ease for an extended period of time.

Again, I don't believe that my problem has ever been with religion. I still believe that my problem is with people and with those who accept the spiritual guidance, regardless of what they're calling it, offered as a weekly handout by clergy. It seems that most of us have already been trained to believe that a church or temple is the only viable source for what we need, while our greatest source is actually found within ourselves. We've always been able to tap into this natural spring simply by helping others.

I understand that nothing I've written here applies to absolutely everybody. I know that, for some, going to a place of worship is simply a matter of habit. For others, it's a matter of keeping up appearances or meeting the supposed expectations of society (though I suspect that a lot of that is only in our heads). There are many who visit their place of worship simply because their spouse or family expects it of them. In any case, there are many who go to their place of worship for all but the obvious reasons.

It is for them that I wish to suggest that this doesn't necessarily mean that they're lost in a theological or spiritual sense. What I'd like to suggest, as an alternative, is that maybe they've grown up. The training wheels need to come off, and their church shouldn't have to do any additional babysitting. Most of these individuals are probably capable of guiding themselves. They should be able to pray or chant to their gods at home, away from the internal bias or uncomfortable opinions of an entire group of followers. All of us should feel free to form a solid relationship with our deity of choice, knowing full well that our creator is going to hear us.

Writing this chapter forces me to remember why and how I finally realized that our need for hope is the true foundation on which almost every religion has been constructed. Hope is the need that I've repeatedly spoken of. Our capacity for hope was the first gift—other than life it-self—that our universe gave to us. When circumstances prove themselves unkind, or when awful things happen that we haven't any control over, we feel our hope snatched away. We aren't supposed to live without it, and I know from personal experience that an absence of hope causes us to do some crazy or stupid shit. This is also when I realized that offering hope to another can help us to restore our own. It is my belief that when our creator made us capable of coherent thought, our source of creation (i.e., the universe) also gave us the capacity for either good, hopeful acts or evil, hopeless ones. It is with this broad capability that we test ourselves each and every day, simply by walking the path that real life has set out for us.

It's true that I assigned the role of creator to the entire universe. I've done that for a few reasons—the main being that this is a legitimate fact. The universe is our one-and-only known source of creation. Whether or not it was created purposely by an intelligent entity is the only notion that requires some faith, but I'm comfortable with this. That a species as complicated as humanity was just a lucky accident seems so unlikely to me that when I pick and choose which of our many deities to pray and offer my thanks to, I know that the source hears me. (I believe that all gods or icons that we speak to are of the source.)

I consider myself one of the Hopeful, and it is this belief that sustains me. I'm discussing a belief in an all-powerful consciousness that exists not only within all of us but also as a part of everything around us. This particular claim to divinity cannot be verified any more than another such claim, but its basic assertions are undeniable.

The first is that hope is a necessity.

The second is that we can gain hope by offering it to others.

The third is that if everybody were willing to help everybody else, most of us probably wouldn't need to.

All I think we should have to do is select the deity we are most comfortable with, be it Brahma, Buddha, Krishna, Dionysus, Zoroaster, or any of the other mythological figures that just happen (as if) to share a few too many things with Jesus Christ. We should pray to this deity every morning and every evening. Being a representative or an icon of the source, we shouldn't need proof that the deity hears us. All we should need to do is share our hopes, dreams, and best wishes with everyone who needs them. That was all I needed. My disability prevented a more active role out in the world, but it never impeded my enthusiasm.

I think my point is that America needs to shift its focus. As a society, we spend far too much time and energy on what keeps us on the fast track into an imagined paradise of full breasts, halos, wings, unlimited pizza, and pearly gates. We are also too focused on not doing what a couple of cranky old douchebags insist will piss off the creator (kinda like I'm doing right now), despite their complete and total lack of inside info on what might be in our creator's head. Instead, we should focus on doing what we can to make life better for those who need our help in the here and now. That applies to everybody.

I might agree that how we live determines where we go after death, but only in the sense that our hopeful, selfless deeds can keep us in the hearts and minds of people we've come to care about. That alone should be all that concerns us, and those who disagree only do so because they're too terrified of death to think either clearly or selflessly.

This is where my preaching ends. What I've shared are the ABCs of me, and I'm comfortable with that. I'm also okay if somebody reads this and decides that mine is a spiritual practice that he or she can adopt for themselves. Go ahead! I just don't wish to accept any responsibility should some deranged fool stop taking medication or decide that one of our creator's many gods or icons has spoken and given him permission to conceive six children from six different women on the sixth of June.

Chapter 10
BALANCE

I'm pretty sure that readers are already aware of one thing for certain, besides the fact that my writing sucks. Just in case it hasn't already been made clear to Joe Average, I'll speak plainly. I am not in any way, shape, or form a capitalist. It wasn't anything personal. Capitalism is a flawed system, and what's truly perverse is that it's the people's very imperfections that perpetuate these flaws. We can't help it, so I forgive most of us.

In my view, capitalism is an economic system that encourages growth, profit, and achievement—but at a terrible cost. In other words, what we have to do is make sacrifices that can hurt our neighbors. In order to make a profit, companies need to fire hundreds of employees and move out of the country. They have to sell fossil fuels and the machines that burn them to sustain an industry that causes harm to our environment, and they do this only because it secures the short-term future of each individual who profits from it. Capitalism turns the human race into a parasitic organism, burning or devouring everything in its path. It is for this reason alone that I reject it and everything it stands for. I choose to turn my back on capitalism—not because I'm un-American or unpatriotic, but because I care for everybody, believe in hope, and reject anything or anybody that makes a habit of taking it away.

Our biggest problem in today's society is balance. Or, to be more specific, balance is our problem because we haven't got any. This lack of balance is mostly caused by skewed priorities that are preserved and protected by the freedoms that we in this country blindly hold so close to our hearts. I haven't any problem with the freedom to survive, the freedom to accomplish something worthy, the freedom to protect or sustain the families we love, and the freedom to live without worry. I have very little cause or reason to object to any of these. The problem that I have is with the types of freedom in the United States of America that have been manipulated. Now we have the freedom to take more than we need at the expense of other people, the freedom to risk our planet and our lives without any accountability, and the general freedom to be thoughtless, inconsiderate assholes.

It doesn't matter what we might call these types of freedom; the fact remains that our lives are not our own. We've allowed ourselves to be controlled by these people and their corporations. Whether or not we realize it, we're being led by the distractions that they've laid out for us. What are we being distracted from? We're being distracted from a global lack of hope.

Regardless of my personal beliefs and how I might have sounded earlier, we're being distracted from any or all indications that our lives are supposed to be better than they've been. Each of us is capable of greatness, but an increasing number of us are falling short. While some may have simply chosen not to live up to expectations, there are others whose chances of success have already been sabotaged, whether or not it was done advertently.

Remember when I suggested that we should determine within ourselves what the differences are between *want* and *need*? I believe that if each of us were to spend time simply making sure that all of our needs were taken care of and that all of our unnecessary wants were ignored, our world and this society would be better for it. I believe that knowing and understanding the difference between the two would bring back a balance in our society that we've not had for quite a while, if ever.

I could be wrong, but I doubt it. The advertisement industry accomplished something truly horrific by blurring the line between *want* and *need* as much as possible. Since commercials tell us we need a smartphone simply because it does everything for us but wipe our asses, we suddenly have to have one. This is despite the cost and what we might have to sacrifice in order to have it. For most of the population, it seems that once a commercial tells us we need something, it's a done deal.

This goes beyond the pocket computers. As with our automobiles, once we develop a great-enough desire for something new, we tailor our lives around it. It abruptly becomes absolutely essential, and we would never survive without it. How many jobs have we applied to that were located over thirty minutes or an hour away by car? Screw walking, right? Okay. And how badly have we panicked when we realized that the cell phone with the GPS was left at home? What's up? Have we forgotten how to read maps?

It's not the toys or distractions that I have a problem with so much as it is the dependency we feel for them. Whether we wish to admit it or not, we've turned ourselves into willing slaves to convenience. We've become subservient to an imagined need for things that we only think we want because our big obnoxiously expensive flat-screen moron-boxes tell us so.

We're facing an inevitable collapse. It's not only a collapse of our society or our way of life but a collapse of everything that we currently believe we need for survival. To be perfectly honest with you, I'm almost of the opinion that the end of this society can't come fast enough, and after writing all of this, why shouldn't I be? We're not losing all of the elements or drives of the human spirit from our collective unconscious; we're allowing these elements to be taken away from us.

I wish to stop talking about this because it's freaking depressing, and I'm aware that most of you are gonna believe I'm just a nut. I wish to suggest that the world isn't ending, but it is going to change. It won't be pretty—especially after we've lost one of our ice caps—and what we do to prepare for it is important. The poor should accept what's left of society but also learn to live outside of it (since it caused most of our problems). Tighter communities should take shape (where the land is not yet underwater), and a large number of us need to read what is not currently in our curricula about wilderness survival. We need to forget just about everything we've been trained or conditioned to believe about how we treat our fellow humans—because not one of us can survive alone.

Now that I've finished writing this, I think I'm going to retire and become a poet.

ABOUT THE AUTHOR

Scott Edward Belbey lives a quiet life with his loving wife and their adorable dog. He hopes to be around to see the world become a better place.

www.ingramcontent.com/pod-product-compliance
Lightning Source LLC
Chambersburg PA
CBHW070508290526
45790CB00003B/1144